A Boy With the
BROKEN HEART

Hello, dear Readers!

I'm Hanna, and I'm thrilled to take you on a journey unlike any other—the story of my son, Yehor—the boy behind Liam's character. This is a true story of courage, hope, and the unbreakable bond between a mother and her child.

In a world of endless diversity, one of the first lessons a child learns is that everyone is different from them. How they respond to this realization depends on what they've been taught and had modeled to them. Do they stare? Laugh? Maybe they even leave, overcome by the discomfort.

The goal of this book is to replace the discomfort of unfamiliarity with curiosity and understanding. Centered around disability, this book lays down a path to understanding through empathy and vulnerability. It teaches that diversity, difference, and individuality are not just traits that we must grow accustomed to but blessings that define the essence of humanity. We are beautiful because we are unique.

As the mother of a boy with a disability, I have seen the difference it makes when my son is understood by strangers; and not only understood, but felt. His pain felt, his desire felt, his innate yearning for more and better felt. It is the embracing of these shared ties that binds us together as humans and gives the world hope of becoming better.

It is in that sacred question: how would I feel if I were in their place?

I invite you to ask yourself this question as you read this story and in doing so, become a member of the Mighty Heart Society.

Let's embark on this transformative journey together, fostering the change-makers of tomorrow!

We've all read stories and seen movies,
With heroes strong and brave.
Men and women who are always there,
When Earth needs to be saved.

Heroes fly in the sky and travel time,
That's what we've been told.
Their lives are filled with mystery,
Adventures cunning and bold.

What movies and books don't tell us,
Is that there are other heroes too.
Their superpowers are harder to see,
But they hold Earth together like glue.

Liam was one of these heroes,
Whose story we now begin.
Life tried each day to tear him down,
But he refused to let it win.

He was born with a heart problem, you see,
And many of his days were spent,
In hospitals with tubes and beeps,
And medicine wherever he went.

He wore a pacemaker all the time,
That guided the rhythm of his heart.
He told the doctors he didn't need it,
But doctors, Mom said, were smart.

Three times he went into surgery,
And his life was under threat,
And three times he gave his heart's enemy,
A lesson it wouldn't forget.

Anyone else would have let go,
And let this sickness beat them,
But Liam was an extraordinary boy,
And nothing could defeat him.

That's what his mother thought at least,
And every day she told him,
That his heart was the strongest heart of all,
And no sickness could hold him.

But each day when he went to school,
He heard whispers and quiet laughter.
He acted as if he didn't mind,
But sometimes he cried after.

Sometimes they didn't mean what they said,
Sometimes they said nothing at all.
Sometimes it was just how they looked at him,
That made his heart fall.

When Liam wanted to join in tag,
They told him he didn't belong,
And when he wanted to play dodgeball,
They said it was for the strong.

Sometimes it was just how they thought,
That he was different from the rest.
How they treated him like he needed help,
Because of the pacemaker on his chest.

He was kind, polite, and funny,
And everyone knew he was smart,
But to his classmates he would always be,
The boy with the broken heart.

He dreamed of becoming an architect,
Making buildings strong and true.
"But if your heart's broken," his classmates said,
"Your buildings will break too!"

Liam tried to shut out their voices,
He tried not to believe them,
But too many voices speaking hurtful words,
Started to deceive him.

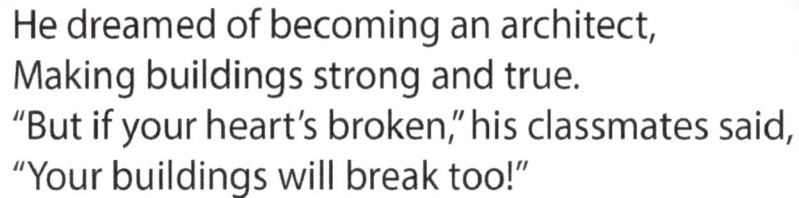

Soon Liam realized,
It wasn't only their voices he heard,
But his own voice in his own head,
Repeating their hurtful words.

He listened to music wherever he went,
Pretending the voice wasn't there.
He hummed and sang, but no matter how loud,
THE VOICE WAS EVERYWHERE!!!

Soon, he noticed something else,
A shadow was following him.
All the doubt and rude assumptions,
Were finally swallowing him.

When he went to play a game of darts,
His shadow spoke to him,
"You're just a boy with a broken heart,
You will never win."

Even when he was in class,
Reading, or taking a test,
His shadow was there to remind him,
Of the pacemaker on his chest.

He tried to get this shadow to go,
He told it to leave him alone,
But the shadow said that it only told him,
Thoughts that were already his own.

One day Liam was walking in the park,
With the closest friend he had.
Her name was Nora and she was there for him,
Whenever things got bad.

"Am I a normal boy?" he asked,
"Or is the voice in my head right?
It says that you need a normal heart,
To live a happy life."

Nora was a hero herself,
She made the world a lovely place.
She handed out hugs and endless love,
And put a smile on every face.

But what made Nora a hero to Liam,
Wasn't anything she did,
But how she treated him like he was normal,
Like any other kid.

He wasn't the boy with the broken heart,
Or the boy with the scarred chest,
He was just Liam, her great friend,
And that's what he liked best.

"Everyone's a bit odd," said Nora.
"Just have a look around."
Liam did what Nora said,
And this is what he found…

There were people walking EVERYWHERE,
Some were short and some were tall.
Some had poofy, fluffy hair,
Some had no hair at all.

There was a man in a wheelchair,
Playing catch with a child,
And a woman missing an arm and a leg,
And somehow they both smiled.

Everyone was odd in some way,
Different from all the rest.
Some had freckles some had crutches,
Liam had a pacemaker on his chest.

"There's no such thing as a normal person," said Nora,
"We can't be all the same.
Eight billion people ALL alike,
Would be just a bit lame!"

Nora's words comforted Liam,
But the shadow wouldn't leave him.
He bravely spoke about it in class,
But no one would believe him.

He told his mother about it too,
And she told him to be strong.
She spoke softly to him when he cried,
And held him when nights were long.

The shadow knew when Liam was lonely,
And when he felt afraid.
It knew how the pacemaker weighed on his chest,
How he felt different when he played.

It whispered awful things in his dreams,
And bothered him every day,
It said, "You'll always be a special boy,
In that bad sort of way!"

One day, Liam was at the hospital,
To get his pacemaker checked.
His Mom was with him and so was his shadow,
As he had learned to expect.

A boy came into the waiting room,
With a wheelchair and a massive frown.
Liam tried to give him a little smile,
But he himself was down.

"What's wrong with you?" asked the boy,
"You look normal enough to me.
Hospitals are for broken people,
People like me, you see."

Liam pulled down the collar of his shirt,
And showed the scars on his chest.
"We're both normal boys," he said,
"As long as we try our best."

"But a normal boy has legs that move," said the boy,
"And feet that run and play.
A normal boy goes to the park or the field,
Not the hospital everyday."

"A normal boy can go up hills,
Without being helped from behind.
A normal boy can sit where he wants,
And not where he's assigned!"

"A normal boy can go to school,
Without his mother pushing him,
And when a normal boy plays basketball,
His friends don't let him win."

"I just want to be normal," he said,
"Climb trees and go up stairs.
Sometimes I ask why it's me,
And not someone else in this awful chair."

"But you're a hero!" Liam said,
"You're a hero, isn't it clear!
Life tries each day to tear you down,
But look at you, you're here!"

"We can sit here and feel sorry for ourselves,
For your legs and for my heart.
We can let this be the end of our story,
Or decide that it's the start."

Liam saw a smile light up the boy's face,
And realized the difference he'd made.
The voice in his head got a little quieter,
And his shadow began to fade.

He left the hospital that day,
With a friend and new belief.
Scars and a pacemaker still sat on his chest,
But a strong heart beat beneath.

Liam realized that everyone has shadows,
That follow them every day.
But if we smiled instead of laughing or judging,
These shadows would go away.

"The world is full of hurting people," he said,
"And there's something I can do.
If I can put a smile on one boy's face,
Why not others too?"

Liam spoke these words to himself,
But something else heard them as well.
His shadow faded even more,
And the voices in his head fell.

Liam called a meeting the next day,
With the strongest heroes he knew.
The boy in the wheelchair, Nora,
And of course, his mother too.

"I've learned something about myself," he said,
"That the world has tried to hide.
My scars and pacemaker can never change,
The heart that beats inside."

"Our strength isn't in muscle or looks,
In our speed or even our smarts,
But in understanding and kindness,
And how we use our mighty hearts."

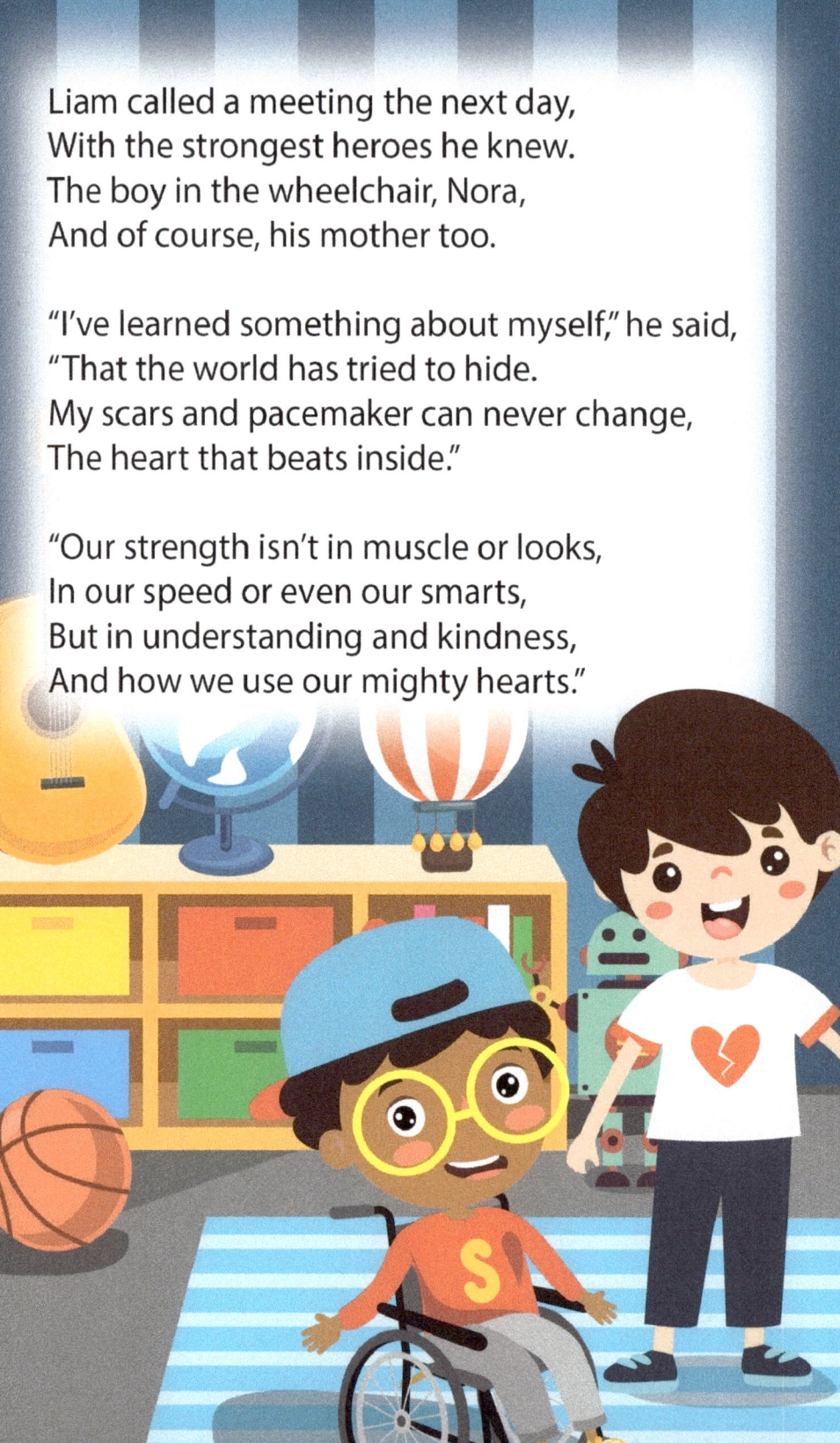

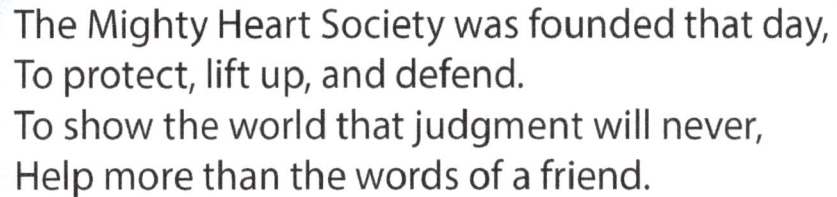

The Mighty Heart Society was founded that day,
To protect, lift up, and defend.
To show the world that judgment will never,
Help more than the words of a friend.

That day, Liam's strength made him forget,
About the things that he once feared.
The voice in his head was gone completely,
And his shadow disappeared.

We're all so busy looking for heroes,
That we forget we're heroes too.
If a boy with a broken heart can change the world,
Why can't me and you?

All it takes is one strong heart,
To keep this world spinning.
The Mighty Heart Society lives on,
This is only the beginning!

Authors Note

Thank you so much for purchasing this book and for meeting Liam.
If you enjoyed it, please leave a review or recommend it to a friend.

Thank you again for your support!
Hanna Nazarenko

Scan the code below to get your free gift now!

www.ingramcontent.com/pod-product-compliance
Lightning Source LLC
Chambersburg PA
CBHW051338120626
46547CB00016B/2596